D0432231

OCT 10

ATOMIC

COWBOY

MARC TYLER NOBLEMAN

Raintree

Chicago, Illinois

Designed by Victoria Bevan and Bigtop
Printed and bound in China by Leo Paper Group

12 11 10 09 08
10 9 8 7 6 5 4 3 2 1

**Library of Congress
Cataloging-in-Publication Data**

Nobleman, Marc Tyler.
  Cowboy / Marc Tyler Nobleman.
      p. cm.
  Includes bibliographical references and index.
  ISBN 978-1-4109-2961-7 (library binding-
hardcover) -- ISBN
978-1-4109-2982-2 (pbk.)
  1. Cowboys--West (U.S.)--Juvenile literature. 2.
West (U.S.)--Social
life and customs--Juvenile literature. 3. Cowboys
in popular culture--United States--Juvenile
literature. 4. Cowboys--Juvenile literature.
5. Cowboys in popular culture--Juvenile literature.
I. Title.
  F596.N63 2008
  978--dc22

                    2007003389

Acknowledgments

The author and publisher are grateful to the
following for permission to reproduce copyright
material: Alamy Images (Stock Connection Blue)
p. **14**; Corbis pp. **6** (Jonathan Blair), **13** (MacDuff
Everton), **20** (top) (Steven Clevenger), **22** (Hubert
Stadler), **18** (Reuters), **26** (top) (Underwood &
Underwood), **29** (Buddy Mays); Getty Images pp. **5**
(The Image Bank), **10** (The Image Bank), **17** (Time
Life Pictures), **20** (bottom) Hulton Archive), **25**
(bottom) (Hulton Archive); Library of Congress p.
25 (top) Vinmag p. **26** (bottom).

Cover photograph of cowboy cattle roping
reproduced with permission of Corbis (David
Stoecklein).

Photo research by Hannah Taylor
Illustrations by Jeff Edwards and Ron Wilson.

The publishers would like to thank Nancy Harris,
Diana Bentley, and Dee Reid for their assistance in
the preparation of this book.

Every effort has been made to contact copyright
holders of any material reproduced in this book.
Any omissions will be rectified in subsequent
printings if notice is given to the publishers.

Disclaimer

All the Internet addresses (URLs) given in this book
were valid at the time of going to press. However,
due to the dynamic nature of the Internet, some
addresses may have changed, or sites may have
changed or ceased to exist since publication. While
the author and publishers regret any inconvenience
this may cause readers, no responsibility for any
such changes can be accepted by either the author
or the publishers.

Contents

Some words are printed in bold, **like this**. You can find out what they mean in the glossary. You can also look in the box at the bottom of the page where the word first appears.

WHAT IS A COWBOY?

A cowboy is someone who looks after cattle. Cowboys usually work on huge farms called ranches. Some ranches have hundreds of cattle. Cowboys must ride horses or drive trucks to keep control of them all.

Ranch owners sell cattle to food companies for meat and milk. Many of our meals would be very different without cowboys!

Exciting shows

Cowboys are also entertainers. They star in shows called **rodeos**. Crowds gasp as cowboys ride wild bulls and horses, and do rope tricks.

cattle	animals such as cows and bulls that are raised for their meat, milk, and hides (skins)
ranch	farm where cowboys raise cattle
rodeo	show in which cowboys perform with horses and cattle

Many ranches are located in the wide-open lands of the southwest United States.

Cowboy fact!

In the United States, cowboys were most common from the 1860s to the 1880s.

Branding means burning
a mark into an animal's skin.
Cowboys use a hot metal bar.

brand	put a mark on cattle to show who owns the animals
market	place where goods and animals are bought and sold
predator	animal that hunts and eats other animals

6

What Do Cowboys Do?

Cowboys need many skills to help run a ranch.

Cowboy jobs

Cowboys feed **cattle**. They take care of sick animals. They protect the animals from coyotes and other **predators**. They bring cattle to **market** and sell them. They do not rest much!

Cowboys **brand** cattle to show who owns the animals. Each ranch has its own brand mark. Not all cowboy duties involve animals. Cowboys also plant crops and fix fences.

Cowboy fact!

People called rustlers try to steal cattle. Luckily, cowboys often stop them.

COWBOY GEAR

Cowboys need more than cattle to do their jobs.

A horse, of course

Cowboys ride horses to **herd** cattle. They sit on saddles to make the ride more comfortable. **Stirrups** are loops that hang off the saddle. Cowboys put their feet in them to stay on the horse.

Spurs are pieces of metal. They are fixed on a cowboy's boots. Horses move forward when they feel the spurs.

Cowboys throw a long rope to catch or hold cattle. The rope is called a **lasso** or lariat. Cattle are strong, so cowboys must also be strong.

Cowboy fact!

Cowboys do not ride the same horse all day. They change horses so the animals can rest.

lasso

saddle

spur

horse

stirrup

herd	move animals from one place to another
lasso	rope used to catch or hold cattle
stirrup	loop where a cowboy puts his foot to help stay on his horse

The wide brims of cowboy hats keep sun and rain out of cowboys' eyes.

COWBOY FASHION

Cowboys may look cool, but they dress to be comfortable.

They wear leather cuffs on their wrists and long-sleeved shirts. These protect their arms from animal scratches and rope burns.

Cowboys sometimes ride near sharp plants such as cacti. They wear leather guards called chaps to protect their legs. Many cowboys wear jeans made of tough material.

Why do cowboy boots have high heels?

Cowboy boots are pointed so that they slip into **stirrups** easily. They have high heels to stop feet from slipping out of the stirrups.

brim	circular piece of material that sticks out at the bottom of a hat

THE CATTLE DRIVE

Ranchers send cattle to market on freight trains. In the 1800s, many ranches were far from a railroad. Cowboys on horseback herded cattle to the trains. These long trips were called cattle drives.

A cowboy year

In the 1800s cattle were not fenced in. They **grazed** (ate grass) wherever they roamed. They roamed on flat, grassy land called **prairies**. Every fall, cowboys rounded up their cattle before the winter storms. In the spring, cowboys chose which cattle to sell. Then, they began the summer cattle drive to the railroad.

freight train	train with railroad cars used to move goods and animals
graze	eat grass, as animals in a field do
prairie	flat, open, grassy land

Today, most ranches are near railroads. Cattle drives are often no longer needed.

Cowboy fact!

Eight to twelve cowboys could drive 2,500 cattle to be sold. It was a moo-ving experience!

A cowboy might get trampled by a bull or bronco if he falls off.

THE RODEO

"Ride 'em, cowboy!", "Don't let go!" You might hear this being yelled at a rodeo.

What are modern rodeos like?

Cowboys on horseback test their skills in front of a crowd. In **calf** roping, cowboys try to catch running calves with a rope. It is called a **lasso**.

Cowboys try to stay on wild horses called **broncos** for at least eight seconds. The broncos try to buck (throw off) the cowboys.

Cowboy fact!

Cowboys also ride bulls. If a bull snags a cowboy's shirt with its horns, the cowboy may need to get the shirt off quickly. That is why some cowboy shirts have snaps instead of buttons.

bronco   horse that has not been trained
calf   young cattle animal

COWBOY LINGO

Cowboys have created their own language. It is a mix of English and Spanish. Today, even people who are not cowboys use cowboy **lingo**.

How do you speak Cowboy?

"Chow" or "chuck" means food. On **cattle** drives, cowboys ate from the chuck wagon that traveled with them. The chef was called a cookie.

When cowboys want to leave, they might say, "Vamoose." This means, "Let's go." They tell their horse to move by saying, "Giddyup!"

Cowboys have other words for "cowboy." They might say "cowpoke," "cowpuncher," or "buckaroo."

Cowboy fact!

To a cowboy, a dead person is not "dead." He is "buzzard food."

If cowboys did not like the meal from the chuck wagon, they might "bellyache." This means complain.

buzzard   bird that eats dead animals

lingo   words used by a certain group, such as cowboys

The Lone Ranger was a TV show about
a cowboy and his Native American friend
Tonto. They fought side by side against
the show's "baddies."

COWBOY MYTHS

Real cowboys are different from many movie cowboys.

What do cowboys use guns for?

Movie cowboys are often involved in gun battles. Some real cowboys carry guns, but not to shoot **outlaws**. Cowboys are **ranch hands**. They work on ranches, they are not police officers. They use a rifle only to scare off **predator** animals.

Good or bad?

In some cowboy movies, cowboys wear white hats. This is a sign that they are good. In real life, cowboys wear any color hat they like.

outlaw	criminal
ranch hand	person who works on a ranch

COWGIRLS

Not all cowboys are male. Female cowboys are often called cowgirls.

Old West cowgirls probably did not go on **cattle** drives. Yet they did tend to cattle on **ranches**. Today, cowgirls do the same jobs as cowboys.

Do cowgirls work at rodeos?

In the early days of **rodeos**, women sometimes competed against men. Today, cowboys and cowgirls are usually in separate rodeo events.

Cowboy fact!

Some cowgirls wear special skirts. They are split so that the cowgirls can sit on a horse.

| Old West | western United States in the second half of the 1800s |

A popular cowgirl rodeo event is barrel racing. Cowgirls on horseback must race around barrels without knocking any over. The fastest rider wins.

These girls were taking part in a rodeo in the 1930s.

Gauchos can be found in much of South America.

BRAZIL

ATLANTIC OCEAN

PACIFIC OCEAN

URUGUAY

ARGENTINA

Countries where gauchos can be found in some areas

0   1,000 miles

0   1,000 kilometers

These gauchos ride in the deserts of Argentina.

COWBOYS AROUND THE WORLD

Where there are cattle, there are usually cowboys.

The first cowboys were Spanish-born Americans.

What are vaqueros and gauchos?

In Mexico a cowboy is called a vaquero. In the 1800s, Americans who moved to Texas learned how to be cowboys from vaqueros. They began to use **lassos** and to **brand** cattle. Soon cowboys spread across the western United States.

In some South American countries, a cowboy is called a gaucho.

FAMOUS COWBOYS

Some cowboys became famous just by doing what they loved.

Bill Pickett invented bulldogging. In this extreme sport, a cowboy would wrestle a **steer**. He grabbed its horns and bit its upper lip!

William Cody created Buffalo Bill's Wild West Show. It was like a circus with cowboy and Native-American acts. The show traveled around the country.

A famous cowgirl

A major star of Cody's show was Annie Oakley. Oakley was an expert **sharpshooter**. A sharpshooter can hit small targets from a distance.

Cowboy fact!

In the 1800s, John Chisum owned 80,000 cattle in New Mexico. He was known as the "Cattle King."

sharpshooter   person who has great aim with a gun

steer   type of male cattle

Bill Pickett was famous for inventing the sport of bulldogging.

THE NORMAN FILM MFG. CO.
PRESENTS

BILL PICKETT
"THE BULL-DOGGER"
Death Defying Feats of Courage and Skill.
THRILLS! LAUGHS TOO!
Produced by NORMAN FILM MFG. CO.
JACKSONVILLE, FLA.

OAKLEY

Annie Oakley was only 5 feet (1.5 meters) tall. A Native-American chief called her "Little Sure Shot."

John Wayne starred in many
westerns. In 1970 he played
the real-life "Cattle King,"
John Chisum.

Readers could enjoy
a new cowboy story
every week!

STREET & SMITH'S

WILD WEST
10¢ WEEKLY
ALL STORIES COMPLETE

MARCH 18
1939

A GUN LAWYER FOR CIRCLE J by Cleve Endicott

COWBOYS IN STORIES

Cowboys have been heroes in all kinds of stories.

How are cowboys described in books and movies?

The first cowboy novels came out in the 1800s. These thrilling tales cost ten cents. Cowboys later appeared in comic books such as *Hopalong Cassidy*.

What is a western?

Cowboy movies and TV shows are called **westerns**. Many movie cowboys are serious. Some cowboys are funny, like Woody from *Toy Story*.

From the 1950s to the 1970s, many westerns aired on TV. One of them, *Gunsmoke*, ran for 20 years!

western   movie or TV show that takes place in the Old West

MODERN COWBOYS

A cowboy's purpose has not changed for more than 150 years. What has changed is the way cowboys do their jobs.

How do cowboys work today?

Cowboys still ride horses. They now drive pick-up trucks, too. They still keep track of **cattle**, but not always by **branding**. Sometimes they put a small electronic **chip** in an animal's ear.

Cowboys are still at home on the **range**. Only now they have more tools to help them.

Cowboy fact!

Even fences have gone high tech. Electric fences lightly shock animals that touch them. Cattle—and predators—learn to stay away.

Cattle are held steady while the chip is put in their ear.

| chip | tiny device that stores information |
| range | large, open area where cattle eat |

Glossary

brand put a mark on cattle to show who owns the animals

brim circular piece of material that sticks out at the bottom of a hat

bronco horse that has not been trained

buzzard bird that eats dead animals

calf young cattle animal

cattle animals such as cows and bulls that are raised for their meat, milk, and hides (skins)

chip tiny device that stores information

freight train train with railroad cars used to move goods and animals

graze eat grass, as animals in a field do

herd move animals from one place to another

lasso rope used to catch or hold cattle

lingo words used by a certain group, such as cowboys

market place where goods and animals are bought and sold

Old West western United States in the second half of the 1800s

outlaw criminal

prairie flat, open, grassy land

predator animal that hunts and eats other animals

ranch farm where cowboys raise cattle

ranch hand person who works on a ranch

range large, open area where cattle eat

rodeo show in which cowboys perform with horses and cattle

sharpshooter person who has great aim with a gun

steer type of adult male cattle

stirrup loop where a cowboy puts his foot to help stay on his horse

western movie or TV show that takes place in the Old West

Want to Know More?

Books

✴ DK Eyewitness Books: *Wild West.* New York: Dorling Kindersley, 2005.

✴ Gibbons, Gail. *Cowboys and Cowgirls: Yippee-Yay!* New York: Little Brown Young Readers, 2003.

✴ Miller, Heather. *This Is What I Want to Be: Cowboy.* Chicago: Heinemann Library, 2002.

Websites

✴ www.nationalcowboymuseum.org/diamondr/
Take a fun tour of a cowboy museum. Play games and find cowboy recipes, puzzles, and much more!

✴ www.cowboyshowcase.com
Learn more about cowboys at this site.

If you liked this Atomic book, why don't you try these...?

Index